TREETOP HIDEAWAYS

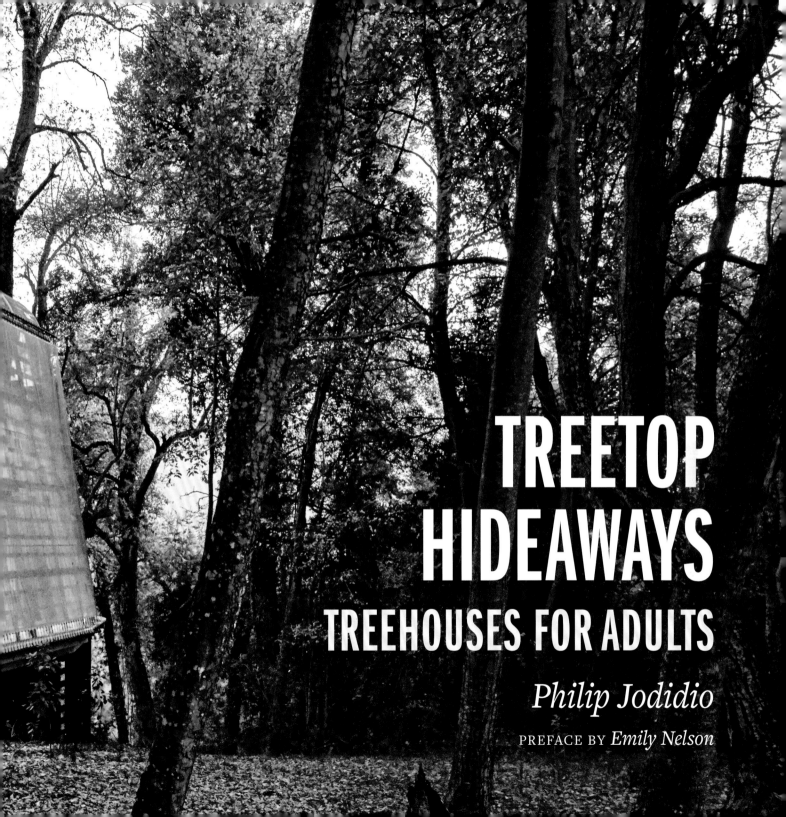

# TREETOP HIDEAWAYS

## TREEHOUSES FOR ADULTS

*Philip Jodidio*

PREFACE BY *Emily Nelson*

# CONTENTS

# Preface
# AT HOME IN THE TREES

EMILY NELSON

**IN 1994, WHEN MY DAD, PETE NELSON**, turned his personal passion for building treehouses into a business, treehouses were vaguely subversive. An outlaw concept, even. Back then, forming a company that specialized in treehouses was not anyone's idea of a smart business plan. But he couldn't resist the joy he found in creating playful spaces in the treetops—and he discovered, to his delight, that treehouses brought joy to others as well.

As time went on, treehouse designs grew in popularity. Soon we were no longer one of only a few treehouse builders in the world—new treehouse companies began to sprout up every year to meet growing demand and make even the wildest treehouse fantasies come true. At the same time, my father and those who followed in his footsteps became interested in how to build *better* treehouses—more structurally sound, more comfortable to spend time in, and safer for the trees that supported them. Our team started collaborating with structural engineers and architects who were interested in low-impact building practices and sustainable materials. We developed new kinds of treehouse hardware, designed to protect and evolve with the host trees. Those original treehouses and host trees are still thriving, almost thirty years later. And regulators have finally caught up with the reality that there is a way to build a treehouse with structural integrity.

Why the treehouse boom? It's the result of a combination of things. For starters, millions have been introduced to treehouses through social media and television shows such as *Treehouse Masters* on Animal Planet and Discovery. More recently, the pandemic inspired many to build treehouses in order to create a sense of adventure and wonder while staying safe at home.

The trend extends beyond the backyard. These days, many businesses are building commercial treehouses. Treehouse vacation rentals and getaways are proliferating, and they draw everyone from couples looking for a romantic retreat to families interested in a one-of-a-kind nature experience for their kids.

And yet, no matter how professionalized and mainstream treehouses become, one thing remains the same: Treehouses are magical. They can be adventurous, whimsical, romantic, rustic, or elegant. No matter the style or function, a treehouse encourages you to step out of the ordinary and into the extraordinary.

There's no limit to what you can build in the trees. We have created secret lairs, reached by hidden staircases, ADA-accessible classrooms, honeymoon getaways with full plumbing, and—one of my personal favorites—a detailed replica of Han Solo's Millennium Falcon, complete with cockpit.

Trees have always occupied a special place in our hearts and imaginations. They are essential to our spirits and continued existence on the planet. It's our hope that the experience of spending time in the trees—becoming attuned to their sounds and subtle movements, taking deep breaths of clean air—will inspire more people to find joy in nature, and join in efforts to protect it.

# PERCHANCE TO DREAM
## *Living the Treehouse Life*

PHILIP JODIDIO

QUESTION: **WHAT DO** treehouses have to do with Airbnb? The answer will not surprise many people. Another question: What are the most wish-listed Airbnb stays in each U.S. state? The answer early in 2021 in Arkansas, Colorado, Georgia, Hawaii, Maine, Mississippi, Montana, New Hampshire, New York, North Carolina, Ohio, Oregon, Texas, Utah was . . . a treehouse. In fact, the most wished-for listing on Airbnb worldwide is the Secluded Intown Treehouse in Atlanta.

So, it isn't an accident that at least one of the most wish-listed treehouses would find its way into this book—Willow, near Woodstock, was the top early 2021 pick for New York. Designed by Antony Gibbon, Willow is in many ways a representative of a new generation of treehouses, precisely because it isn't exactly a treehouse. In the era of glamping, any self-respecting treehouse seems to need electricity and running water and—sure, why not?—nearly 600 square feet (56 square meters) of luxurious interior space. Willow breaks other rules; it doesn't hang from a tree, but instead touches the ground lightly at just three points. The treehouse is morphing into a luxurious hotel room in the air. Several treehouses in this book are in this category, or at least can be counted amongst the many forest lodgings offered by "eco-resorts" around the world.

## FROM THE MEDICI TO DISNEYLAND

It is thought that some early humans lived in trees for obvious reasons of self-protection, much as others chose caves. And so, trees and caves can be counted amongst the most obvious sources of residential design. Early men wanted to get away, not from the stress of urban life, but instead from bears and unpleasant neighbors. The idea of being in the trees for more pleasant, relaxing reasons came as early as Roman times and was certainly well established by the era of the Medici. The Grand Duke of Tuscany Cosimo de' Medici (1519–1574) created a treehouse at the Villa di Castello (Florence, 1538) with a concealed fountain system intended to soak unsuspecting visitors. This inspired his son Francesco de' Medici (1541–1587) to build another treehouse in a holm oak 25 feet (7.6 meters) above the ground with two spiral staircases at the Villa di Pratolino (Vaglia, 1581).

It would be tedious to cite the treehouses that have dotted reality and fiction since the time of the Medici, but in more recent times, again, it is no accident that the Swiss Family Treehouse is an attraction at Disneyland in Tokyo and Paris and Disney World in Florida. This presence is, of course, linked to the 1960 film *Swiss Family Robinson* and further back to the 1812 novel of the same name by Johann

The Willow Treehouse, designed by Antony Gibbon and located near Woodstock, New York, seeks to resolve a real problem faced by some getaways of this type—how to be resolutely contemporary and offer a modicum of comfort while also being respectful of the natural environment and fitting into a wooded site.

11

David Wyss. In that story, a shipwrecked family builds an elaborate treehouse as their home on a deserted island. The American fascination with treehouses can be traced at least partially to these fictional adventures. The idea of escape—be it out of revolt against the polluted modern world, or merely a romantic ideal of a simpler life, even for a few days—is deeply ingrained in the minds and hearts of today's growing number of treehouse devotees. Treehouse dreams are most probably free of bugs, creaking wood, and being an awfully long way down to the ground. Nonetheless, recent hopes to flee the pandemic-ridden world have driven a nearly global passion for sleeping far away from other modern risks and perils.

## TREEHOUSE MASTERS

Two different directions are apparent in the treehouses published here. One is that of increasing comfort and modernity, including running water, electricity, and Wi-Fi, as well as construction based on sophisticated materials and equipment used in other forms of contemporary architecture. In the United States, numerous firms offering professional treehouse construction services have prospered. These are along the lines of Nelson Treehouse, which was established in 2010 and featured in the reality television series *Treehouse Masters*, aired on Animal Planet and Discovery from 2013 to 2018. Pete Nelson may be the best-known treehouse builder in the world. His Ananda treehouse is published here, and his daughter, Emily, penned the preface of this book. Other firms specializing in tree-borne structures include Dustin Feider's O2; Artistree, which was founded by Will Beilharz; Nid Perché (perched nest), which is based in Sainte-Sabine, France; and Andreas Wenning's German firm baumraum.

The work of such firms as Nid Perché invites commentary about the surprising degree of architectural diversity that exists within the genre. The Châteaux dans les Arbres, located in the Périgord region, for example, transpose the weighty castles of French history into luxurious wooden treehouses connected to a spa. The connection between real castles and these somewhat rusticated avatars, of course, is the stuff of dreams. The French in their own parlance refer to a *château en Espagne* when imagining an impossible project. This expression originated in the historic fact that there are few if any Spanish castles in the countryside of the sort that a Frenchman might one day buy. Simply put, a *château en Espagne* is a pipe dream. And yet it does reveal the underlying fascination held in France and elsewhere for castles. The romantic vision of history that this implies has been readily translated into treehouses that evoke castles in the air. Solid stone becomes less sturdy wood, somehow offering a more down-to-earth way to obtain another French dream—*la vie de château*, or a life of luxury.

## UNIQUE DESIGNS

Despite the arrival of specialized treehouse design firms around the world, it is interesting to note that designs remain very individualized and are often quite original. Artistree, for example, created the Playa Viva treehouse in Zihuatanejo, Mexico, using locally sourced materials in an architecturally very open style made possible by the warm climate on-site. Part of a luxury eco-resort, the treehouse has a floor area of 700 square feet (65 square meters), making it one of the biggest treehouses in this volume. It is almost as though, by their very nature, and their relation to natural settings, treehouses have to be designed to be different from case to case. Precisely because treehouse fans are seeking to get away from more industrialized or standardized environments, they, too, are looking for unique designs. A given tree or series of trees also has a way of imposing its own logic on any structure. It would be very difficult indeed to mass-produce real treehouses, and that makes treehouses different even from such fashionable ideas as the "tiny house." Real handmade structures are also by definition different from case to case, but even successful treehouse design firms have rather consistently sought to make each of their realizations unique.

Playa Viva in Mexico is suspended from beachside palm trees. It was designed by Will Beilharz (Artistree) and is big enough for a king-size bed and a connected bathroom. Made in good part with bamboo, its tubular form guarantees both privacy and open horizons.

In a logical development from the design and construction of individual treehouses, several firms have been at the origin of resorts such as Nelson's TreeHouse Point, which is in Fall City, Washington. Indeed, eco-resorts around the world have become one of the driving forces behind the expansion and multiplication of treehouses. Clearly put, these treehouses are rented by the night like hotel rooms, whence a demand for modern comfort, ranging from kitchens to bathrooms, often perched, like the bedrooms, high in the air. As noted, Airbnb has also become a significant purveyor of treehouse nights, as it were.

## BIRD HUT HOTEL

A variation on the theme of professionally designed treehouses can be found in the unique forms imagined by architects. Examples in this book include the Bird Hut in Windermere, British Columbia, by the interdisciplinary firm Studio North. By carefully studying the habits of local birds, Studio North created a treehouse that resembles a nest itself while providing shelter to twelve different kinds of birds. This design combines professional architectural experience with a real, if somewhat whimsical, expression of ecological concerns. Treehouses are not always respectful of their natural surroundings, but in this instance, the designers are being proactive, seeking to shelter birds as well as humans. Woodsman's Treehouse in the United Kingdom is another hybrid example of the kind of new structure that can be designed when engineers (in this instance bridge designers) get together with an owner who has created a "woodland retreat" in Dorset. The quality of this design is such that it received the 2017 RIBA (Royal Institute of British Architects) South West Small Project of the Year award. Another example of innovative treehouse design carried forward by architects, in this case, the Paris-based firm Atelier Lavit, is Origin, located in a treehouse complex next to the Château de Raray in the Oise region of France. The modern design inspired by the construction of actual bird nests includes running water and electricity, thus bridging the apparent gap with the professional designs by firms specifically dedicated to treehouses.

## GLULAM AND PINECONES

Woodnest was built in 2020 on a steep slope above the Hardangerfjord in Odda, Norway. The two structures concerned were designed by the Norwegian architects Helen & Hard. Decidedly modern in appearance, the buildings were formed with radial glulam timber ribs, and like more traditional treehouses, they are supported by their respective host trees using steel collars. Referencing traditional vernacular timber architecture, Helen & Hard

partially covered the structures with untreated shingles. Since the upper range of the treehouse is in glass, modernity is the governing mode, a fact also attested to by the presence of bathrooms and kitchens. With a floor area of only 161 square feet (15 square meters) each and enough space to sleep four, Woodnest is also an exercise in the design of a kind of tiny house, another very popular idea in circles concerned with the husbanding of resources, both natural and manufactured.

Another architect-designed treehouse published here is the Pigna, built by Claudio Beltrame in Malborghetto, Italy. Consisting of a panoramic covered terrace and an upper-level living space inspired by the form of the pinecone, Pigna was built with cross-laminated timber, wood fiber insulation, and larch shingles. Although it has a kitchen and bathroom, Pigna clearly references ecological concerns and seeks to combine a modern appearance with rough-hewn wood elements and a design intended to disappear into the forest. The lack of a foundation in this and most of the other realizations in this book does, of course, speak to the respect for natural settings. Most treehouses can readily be dismantled without undue loss of materials such as wood—which can be reused if so desired. This is not quite the same as saying that a treehouse must inevitably be an ecologically responsible structure, but it is more likely to perform well in that respect than most traditional homes built with foundations and often with polluting materials. And so, a treehouse offers its residents real proximity to nature at the same time as it acts in a more responsible way vis-à-vis the environment—a double advantage that also explains part of the genre's popularity.

## AN IMAGE OF NATURE

On occasion treehouses can offer architects an opportunity to create innovative structures. Such might well be the case of La Invernada, which was built by Guillermo Acuña Arquitectos Asociados in Curicó, Chile, in the midst of a private 1,483-acre (600-hectare) native forest reserve at 2,600 feet (nearly 800 meters) above sea level. The

Woodnest is a set of tree treehouses located near Odda, Norway. Although the structures reference the traditions of local timber architecture, they are decidedly modern, and include a bathroom, kitchen, and space to sleep four.

rounded, luminous 581-square-foot (54-square-meter) structure was built with laminated CNC (computerized numerical control)-milled Chilean pinewood, 0.3-inch (8-millimeter) monolithic flexible polycarbonate, and an exterior tensile mesh membrane. The structure took just twenty days to build. The architect explains, "We wanted to experiment with the 'vegetal' as the working theme for the design, so the house had to respond to the attributes of nature: light (photosynthesis); fabric (leaves); and wood (trees). The project was conceived as an object that doesn't belong to the site, that can disappear at any time, and that speaks to us of the transitory condition of

occupation of the forest. Transparency evokes this impermanence as it reflects the projected shadows of the forest and their movements during the day on its skin. The textile layer takes on the role of tinting the light gold (the color of the oak leaves in the fall) during the day and acting as a 'sacrificial' cover during storms, protecting the tent from branches that could crack the second layer, which protects the structure from the rain." This deeply natural setting is thus put into contrast with a very modern design, created using the latest techniques and yet still fully respectful of its environment.

On some occasions even a few of the best-known or largest architectural firms in the world are tempted by the idea of designing a unique structure in the trees. This is the case of the 7th Room, created by the Oslo firm Snøhetta for Treehotel in Harads in northern Sweden. Snøhetta, designer of the Alexandria Library and the National September 11 Memorial Museum Pavilion in New York, worked with an area of just 592 square feet (55 square meters) in this case. The architects called on sources of inspiration like a traditional Nordic cabin, creating a wooden façade clad with charred pine boards. Despite the compact nature of the design, the 7th Room is a veritable hotel suite that can accommodate up to five people and includes two bedrooms, a lounge, a bathroom, and a terrace.

## ARTIST OF THE STARS

The second major direction in recent treehouse design and construction has in reality been a continuation of past practices. As opposed to the sophisticated, and often comfortable, designs that have spread across the globe, there are also many treehouses that are very much handmade. These are unique realizations carried forward sometimes by their owners, or instead by professional treehouse designers who favor what might be termed greater authenticity. An outstanding figure in this category is Roderick Wolgamott, who has built more than fifty treehouses across the world. His firm, Romero Studios/Wolgamott Works, designed and built treehouses for the likes of Police front man Sting and his wife, Trudie Styler, the actors Julianne Moore and Val Kilmer, and Donna Karan, the founder of the DKNY fashion label. Wolgamott was a founder of the Seattle band Sky Cries Mary, whence surely his familiarity with stars of music, film, and fashion. Romero Studios uses 98 percent reclaimed or salvaged materials and always tries to collaborate with local craftsmen. Wolgamott's treehouses often feature surprising sculptural accumulations of branches that certainly give a hint that these realizations are something akin to works of art.

Another example of what can be called the handmade trend in treehouses is Urnatur, located in southern Sweden. The Air Castle was made from wood responsibly harvested in the neighboring forest. Urnatur co-founder Ulrika Krynitz makes clear that this and other treehouses in her eco-treehouse lodge are intended for viewing nature and include neither toilets nor kitchens, neither running water nor electricity. This choice is related much less to issues of cost than it is to a real sense of ecology and respect for nature and more specifically for biological diversity.

## OF HORSES AND DRAGONS

Further around the world, the noted Japanese designer Takashi Kobayashi, a former clothing buyer who has been building in trees since 1993, also privileges a clearly artistic esthetic sense together with a comprehension of quality. A measure of Kobayashi's reputation is that two of his realizations published here were built to commemorate significant events in Japan—the hoped-for 2020 Olympic Games in the case of the Equestrian Park treehouse and the terrible Tohoku earthquake for the Tree Dragon, built in Higashi-Matsushima, one of the towns devastated by the post-earthquake tsunami on March 11, 2011. The Tree Dragon is a surprising hybrid, combining a kind of cave with a space that rises to a height of 30 feet (9 meters) off the ground. This is a place of contemplation or even prayer—a treehouse that is deeply connected to

Tree Dragon is an unexpected, three-level organic design imagined by the Japanese treehouse master Takashi Kobayashi. It was built in Japan as a symbol of the country's recovery from the devastating 2011 Tohoku earthquake and tsunami.

instead have become a refuge of a different sort in the modern era. Rather than being artificially imposed on the surface of the earth, they are most often suspended high above the ground, not only declaring their independence from more polluting forms of construction but also offering a sensation of hovering, of being one with the natural world. Where some decry the culture of waste that seems to rule the world, the treehouse is usually small and reductive in its image of consumption and daily life. Foster Huntington, the creator of the Cinder Cone, speaking of his own treehouse, says, "This is small, like 200 square feet. So, it forces you to be a lot more specific about the stuff you have." As for other architectural forms that survive at the periphery of urban development, such as mountain cabins, modern life does somehow find its way into the culture of treehouses. As "specific about the stuff" as he wants to be, Huntington has decided that high-speed internet is part of what he needs way up in the trees, while others look for hot and cold running water, a kitchen, and, why not, a television. This might be thought of as having your cake and eating it, too. Let's get away from the modern world but bring all the creature comforts with us, so to speak.

## THE JUNGLE IS YOUR HEAD

Perhaps Huntington's choice of internet to accompany him is indicative of other, deeper trends in modern life. How many times do we see couples or families in a restaurant, individually immersed in their cell phones? Whether it consists of writing to a distant or even imaginary friend, playing a mind-numbing game, or doing work, internet immersion is sadly a symptom of a somehow desired loneliness that is also an escape from the modern world—plunging down the rabbit hole of virtual reality. So, is it to escape from this kind of modernity that people want to inhabit or visit treehouses, or are those visits an extension of an apocalyptic societal rupture that is playing out everywhere? The answer, of course, lies with the

this place and its recent history. The Japanese tradition of woodworking as an art form is not far from this kind of concept, nor is the tiny space usually allotted to the tea ceremony. Terunobu Fujimori, a noted architect and a former professor of modern Japanese architectural history, is perhaps best known for some of his designs for the teahouses in trees.

## SPECIFIC ABOUT STUFF

Treehouses elicit a broad range of reactions to contemporary life and are deeply rooted in human history. At first a shelter from predators and natural threats, trees individuals who want to sleep 25 feet off the ground. Are they there to reconnect, to disconnect, or to lose themselves in a vertiginous rise that surely implies an equally catastrophic fall? The Irish band U2 performed an evocative tune called "Vertigo" on their 2004 album, *How to Dismantle an Atomic Bomb*:

> *Lights go down, it's dark*
> *The jungle is your head, can't rule your heart*
> *A feeling's so much stronger than a thought*
> *Your eyes are wide and though your soul, it can't be bought*
> *Your mind can wander*
> *Hello, hello (hola)*
> *I'm at a place called Vertigo (¿dónde está?)*
> *It's everything I wish I didn't know*

## FLIRTING WITH TRANSIENCE

Where modern society had promised all kinds of comfort and security, reality is much more worrisome and dangerous. The heights of the treehouse are also a way of flirting with transience and the sense of vertigo procured when looking over the abyss. The point is that treehouses can be viewed or interpreted in many ways, most of them apparently delightful—like a series of Instagram hashtags, #nature #wanderlust #adventure #offgridliving #environmentalsustainability #dreambiglivetiny #warmandcosy. All of these, by the way, are genuine Instagram hashtags that come up when searching for treehouses. But do treehouses have a more negative, even a darker side? Is their popularity also an indication of the discomfort that modern life generates? Is going to a treehouse playful escapism or a desperate need for something else—that call of not only nature but of a long-lost and surely imagined past? *Et in Arcadia ego.* Are treehouses possibly a metaphor for modern life, the one we desperately want to get away from to an imagined better place, hopefully with a nice bathtub and, oh dear, internet? Climb as high as you want, you can't escape.

Both in their occasional use and in their very nature, treehouses seem to run contrary to one of the more sought-after qualities of architecture—its solidity. Treehouses, with very few exceptions, are by nature ephemeral. They need to be light structures just to stay up in a tree, and a tree grows and dies, sometimes nearly as fast as a person. An attraction to the ephemeral and light may be closely related to perceptions of the contemporary world, where changes occur rapidly and nothing seems to remain in place for very long. Where a concrete house is firmly anchored in the earth and may well offer reliable shelter from most of the vicissitudes of nature, trees move in the wind and some treehouses are very poorly insulated. Much of architecture has an underlying tendency to try to deny the real world or to close it out; the treehouse has much more difficulty keeping out the forces and sounds of nature. It is somehow much closer to reality even when it is sold as an escape.

## NOT THE SUNRISE AND THE DAWN MERELY

Coming, as they do, closer to nature, treehouses also imply relatively limited social interaction. Made ideally for two and rarely big enough for more than six, these are places of escape and not of gathering. Again, this has had advantages in a time of pandemic, but it also expresses the desire, or even the need, of many to isolate themselves from others. The idea is to get away from urban sprawl, perhaps, but also somehow from others, crowds, and mass transport, too. Rather than to dwell on the negative aspects that the race to the trees may imply, better surely to stay with the dream of being closer to nature, the Swiss Family Robinson picture of bliss—oh dear, even that is bliss after a shipwreck. Stanching the non-stop flow of information of varying degrees of significance, the treehouse (or at least the one without Wi-Fi and TV) allows some to contemplate the world and themselves, recalling the words of Henry David Thoreau, "To anticipate, not the sunrise and the dawn merely, but, if possible, Nature herself!" ▪

The Air Castle is in southeastern Sweden. It is distinguished by its spiraling stairways and high perch, 20 feet (6 meters) off the ground. It has neither electricity nor water.

# AIR CASTLE

**URNATUR IS AN** eco–treehouse lodge founded by the couple Håkan Strotz and Ulrika Krynitz in a forest outside the town of Ödeshög in the county of Östergötland in southern Sweden. It is 160 miles (260 kilometers, or a three-hour drive) southeast of Stockholm. The Air Castle, one of a group of cabins and treehouses on the site, was built by Strotz about 20 feet (6 meters) above the ground, exclusively with materials from the neighboring forest. It has an area of just 81 square feet (7.5 square meters) and sleeps two (no children allowed) in a 63-inch (160-centimeter)-wide bed. The structure is reached by a spiral staircase attached to a pine tree that leads up to a veranda. A further ladder goes up to a gazebo on the roof of the treehouse. A separate platform is reached via a suspension bridge, offering views of the surrounding forest and pastureland. Krynitz explains, "We try to use only the most natural materials available. All the wood (aside from larch) is from the surrounding forest and is individually harvested with a mind to nature conservation. The houses are very simple (no electricity, no kitchen, no water or toilet inside). They are intended only for observing nature and for sleeping but are equipped with a wood-stove to provide warmth. Experiencing and reconnecting to nature is important to us, as is the whole concept of the place: a holistic farm where the main goal is to maximize biodiversity. Tourism makes it possible to live on the farm and maintain its cultural and biological values even today." In terms of its design and construction, the Air Castle represents what one might call a "primitive" vision of the treehouse—not in any negative sense, but because of the handmade nature of the structure, the lack of utilities, and the very real proximity to nature. Too high, and thus potentially dangerous, for children, it is very much a treehouse for adults—a romantic getaway or a privileged place to observe nature from a higher point. ▪

With its spiraling staircase, suspended bridge, and octagonal viewing platform, Air Castle comes as close as possible to the kind of treehouse that people dream about, even if it pointedly avoids modern comforts.

20

# ANANDA

**TREEHOUSE POINT** is an overnight retreat center in Fall City, Washington. Fall City is located 25 miles (40 kilometers) east of Seattle. The center was created in 2006 by Pete Nelson and his wife, Judy, and now has seven treehouses. Nelson, now accompanied in his work by his three adult children, has built over 350 treehouses around the world and has published his projects frequently. Low-impact building processes and environmental sustainability are quite naturally part of the family ethos. Built in 2020, after four years of planning, the Ananda treehouse, the last treehouse that will be built on the site, is set 25 feet (7.6 meters) above the ground on a steel platform supported by two fir trees. It is covered with cedar shingles laid in what the designer calls a "swingle" pattern. The inside is paneled in reclaimed redwood and Douglas fir. Because of its sloping site and approach bridge, the Ananda treehouse is ADA (American Disabilities Act)–compliant, or wheelchair accessible, despite being very much in the trees. It overlooks the Raging River, which is reputed for fishing, through floor-to-ceiling glazing. The house has a king-size bed, a half bath, a toilet, and a private deck. The Ananda treehouse has a propane fireplace that is "wood-stove inspired." Clearly, although it is very much a treehouse, Ananda comes with many of the comforts of home, including electricity. As Pete Nelson explains, ananda is a cannabinoid that is naturally produced by the brain, producing a state of bliss. In Hinduism, Buddhism, and Jainism, ananda is a term for extreme happiness, one of the highest states of being. Although it is a unique structure built essentially on-site, the Ananda treehouse is witness to the very specialized team that works on Nelson's treehouses. Based on careful planning, it was built by treehouse professionals, offering substantial advantages, in terms of real accessibility in a wilderness setting, and modern comfort. ▪

The Ananda treehouse is easily accessible on the entrance side but is suspended over a steeply sloped site. It has modern comforts and was designed to be wheelchair accessible, a rare feature in treehouses.

# BANANA SLUG MOUNTAIN

**CALLED THE BANANA SLUG MOUNTAIN** Equilibrium Home, this 210-square-foot (19.5-square-meter) treehouse is set 25 feet (7.6 meters) off the ground in Woodside, California. Located in San Mateo County, Woodside is one of the wealthiest small towns in the United States The treehouse is perched amongst California redwoods and was built with redwood, Douglas fir, and prefabricated birch plywood panels in 2017. Although the treehouse has a relatively "traditional" overall appearance, it is apparent from its triangulated structure that more modern ideas are at work. O2 Treehouse, the builder, is based in Oakland, California. The firm was created in 2005 in Pewaukee, Wisconsin, where its founder, Dustin Feider, built his first geodesic structure. The firm's team includes an architect and an industrial designer, as well as experienced woodworkers and builders. Feider explains that the Banana Slug Mountain house is based on a building system that includes a modular treehouse foundation (Tetratruss) and structurally insulated panels that are prefabricated and shipped to the site ready to install. The treehouse has a high-peaked ceiling that leaves space for a loft with a "hide-a-bed" for two, as well as another bed on the lower level. This arrangement provides enough space for four—the beds can be stored to allow for lounge space during the day. Glass doors and an outdoor terrace make the link to the natural setting a constant presence. The Banana Slug Mountain treehouse has a water cistern–fed copper kettle sink and a composting toilet. The builder warns that "you will most likely need directions to the bathroom in this unique treehouse, however, as the bathroom is accessed via a faux built-in bookshelf. Give it a tug and watch as the secret is revealed, exposing the water closet beyond." ▪

Built amongst the California redwoods, the Banana Slug Mountain treehouse combines a rugged wooden structure with a modern triangulated design, making it particularly stable and solid.

# BIRD HUT

**THE BIRD HUT** was built in 2017 by the interdisciplinary Calgary firm Studio North in Windermere, which is in southeastern British Columbia. As its name implies, the structure was designed with an eye to providing nesting for local bird species. As well as accommodating two people, the hut has twelve incorporated birdhouses, each intended for a different type of bird. The sizes and openings of the birdhouses were carefully studied to attract pileated woodpeckers, warblers, and other varieties. The habits of birds are also the reason that the hut is located 9 feet (2.7 meters) off the ground, with its peak 11 feet (3.4 meters) higher. Again, in keeping with the nesting habits of birds, the materials for the structure were scavenged from the immediate surroundings. The cross-braced structure was built with lodgepole pines (Pinus contorta) found in a nearby forest area that had been subjected to fire. The platform and cladding were made with planks reclaimed from the deck of an old cabin. According to the studio, the front façade "is clad with Western red cedar shingles cut with a custom rounded profile, the radii of which were determined by the size of the birdhouse openings and the width of each shingle." The 100-square-foot (9.3-square-meter) structure has a roof made of 0.3-inch (8-millimeter) polycarbonate panels that is intended to provide some heat through a greenhouse effect and two operable round windows. Visitors connect to a spring and a campfire area along an access bridge and a stone path. The variety of designs of treehouses is probably as great as that of more substantial homes, but in this instance, an awareness of ecological concerns is combined with a whimsical view of the world of birds. ▪

The Bird Hut has a whimsical appearance that belies a very real concern for the environment in which it is built—it is not only for people, but also provides a home to various indigenous birds.

# BLACK CRYSTAL

**THE GERMAN DESIGNER** Andreas Wenning (baumraum) is surely one of the best-known treehouse designers in Europe. His style varies but tends very clearly to modern forms. The Black Crystal, built in the Catskills near Woodstock in 2020, is no exception. Its faceted, dark form is indeed quite unexpected in the wooded environment where it is located. The windows and steel structure, including sheet metal for the façades, were prefabricated in Germany and shipped to New York. A local firm, along with a carpenter called Catskill Bill, assembled the remaining timber elements. The 99-square-foot (9-square-meter) oak interior offers a warm and welcome contrast from the black exterior of the structure. A geometric pattern of oak profiles is used for the walls and ceiling. A fixed sofa opens to form a large bed. Supported by an oak, the galvanized, powder-coated steel structure uses four inclined steel supports beneath the cabin, as well as steel cables and textile belts bearing part of the load from above. The terrace is set nearly 14 feet (4.2 meters) above the ground, and the total height of the treehouse is just under 30 feet (9 meters). This ample height gives a real impression of space inside, not a frequent feature of treehouses. The 140-square-foot (13-square-meter) galvanized steel terrace is clad in FSC (Forest Stewardship Council)-certified ipe wood. The insulated façades are made with oak and plywood with a wood frame clad in 0.7-inch (18-millimeter) OSB (oriented strand board) and external cladding in Rimex, highly polished black stainless steel that reflects the surrounding trees. ▪

Although it is not suspended in the trees, the Black Crystal, standing on steel supports, offers all the dreaminess and excitement of the real thing, with modern solidity and lightness in the bargain.

# CABANE HAUTEFORT

**AT THE DOMAINE** de Puybeton in Nojals-et-Clotte, a small town in the Dordogne region of southwestern France, visitors can discover very unexpected Châteaux dans les Arbres (Castles in the Trees). As the name implies, these are no ordinary treehouses. Instead, they are almost full-sized residences set above the ground, their exterior design clearly inspired by the legendary castles of France. The Cabane Hautefort is the largest structure in the group and can sleep from two to six persons. There are three bedrooms with double beds and a fully equipped kitchen with an "American" refrigerator, dishwasher, microwave, and coffee-machine. Wi-Fi, TV, heating, and air-conditioning, and even a year-round spa for six persons, are all part of this very ample and generous design. The wooden cabin has a floor area of no less than 495 square feet (46 square meters), along with a 441-square-foot (41-square-meter) terrace. This is a rather grand expression of the recent trend seen throughout the world, but in particular in Europe and the United States, to create treehouse domains that are used most often in a bed-and-breakfast arrangement. In this instance the unusual idea of the designers on this site, which is 100 miles (160 kilometers) from the city of Bordeaux, has been to echo French tradition while also offering modern comfort to an extent rarely seen in the trees. ▪

The Cabane Hautefort seeks to combine two very different types of structures—a treehouse and a castle, one apparently relatively ephemeral and light, the other, which guides the style but not the materials here, built with stone to last for centuries.

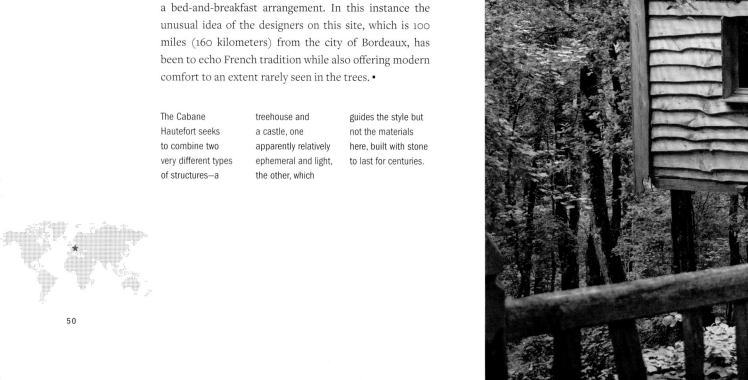

# CHÂTEAU MILANDES

**LOCATED LIKE THE CABANE** Hautefort in the 27-acre (11-hectare) Domaine de Puybeton, Château Milandes is a bit more rustic in its finishing than its larger neighbor. Milandes, which spans a moat, sleeps two to four persons and has one king-size bed, as well as bunkbeds for children. A bathroom with a shower and a Nordic bath on the terrace are part of the scheme. Built in 2012, like Hautefort, Milandes has a floor area of 280 square feet (26 square meters) and an outdoor terrace of the same size. The height of the structure is 26 feet (8 meters). These "castles" in the trees were each designed by a specialized firm called Nid Perché (Perched Nest), which is based in Sainte-Sabine, France, and has built one thousand treehouses and wooden cabins in the past sixteen years. Exterior cladding of the Château Milandes is in Douglas fir and larch. The frame is made of oak, floors are in chestnut, and other wood surfaces are in poplar. Architecturally speaking, it is most unusual to imagine transposing the design of old castles, which were, of course, mostly built of stone, into wood. Perched in trees and provided with modern comfort, these "castles in the trees" are full of historical and architectural contradictions. What castles have in common with treehouses is that both make people dream of another time and place, an escape from the modern world, which, in this instance, doesn't really oblige them to leave behind creature comforts. ▪

Again mixing French tradition and treehouse style, Milandes takes a rustic wooden approach to the image of the fabled castles of Europe.

## THE CINDER CONE

SKAMANIA COUNTY, WASHINGTON, USA · *Foster Huntington*

**THE BUILDER OF THE** Cinder Cone, Foster Huntington, writes, "I left my job in New York in the summer of 2011 and moved into a camper. Since then, I have driven 100,000 miles around the West, surfing and camping. During the summer of 2014, I set up a home base in the Columbia River Gorge." It was in this location in Skamania County, Washington, that he built two treehouses connected by an arching suspended walkway, a soaking tub, and a skate bowl. The structures were built with the help of friends, some of whom were professional carpenters. Huntington, who is a social media consultant, blogger, and photographer, told *The New York Times*, "I could've bought a house. But this is so much better. For me, it's realizing a childhood dream." As it happens, his family owns the land where the treehouses were built, used in earlier years for camping. He explained to the journal *Mpora*, "There's this really cool row of Douglas fir trees on top of the hill, so I thought, 'Hey that's a good spot to build a treehouse, right there with the best view,' so that's what we did." Each of the structures has an area of about 220 square feet (20 square meters), and Huntington uses one of them, equipped with 4G internet, as his home. He said, "I feel like it's important to live in a place that's really inspiring to live and, in this day, and age of the internet, you can kind of work from wherever." The designer emphasizes that living in a small space obliged him to make restrictive choices about the objects he wanted around him, and he also underlines the inclusive nature of parts of the project, such as the skate bowl. Huntington published a crowd-funded book about the Cinder Cone and has received ample internet coverage of his project. ▪

Many treehouses are imagined as places to get away from other people. Foster Huntington, designer of the Cinder Cone, instead made a convivial home and workplace, with space for friends.

# COCO

**COCO IS A GROUP** of five pods that are part of an "art villas" complex located on a 6-acre (2.5-hectare) tropical jungle site in Uvita, Costa Rica, near a Pacific Ocean beach. The owner of the site, Filip Žák, states, "Since I was a young boy, I've been fascinated with treehouses. I watched TV shows about treehouse construction, read every book on treehouses I could get my hands on, and searched the internet for that perfect treetop abode. Very little of what I saw fit my taste until I found a Taschen book about treehouses and discovered French designer Benoît Fray. His concept behind treehouses in Switzerland is, to say the least, extraordinary." In all due modesty, the author of these lines also wrote the Taschen book, published in 2012. Since Fray was not available, Filip Žák turned instead to a Czech firm called Archwerk, which produced Coco. The firm used local tropical wood, a seven-layer tent canvas, and some metal elements without further decoration. The equally spare, essentially tan and white, interiors of the five small Coco buildings were designed by another Czech firm, Formafatal. The design team of Formafatal created wooden footbridges and stairs made of wood and expanded metal-mounted steel columns and platforms for viewing the lush surrounding vegetation and the ocean. The focal point of each of the pods, which are oriented to the best views, is a bed, except for the largest structure, which houses a shared kitchen and dining area. Completed in June 2020, the complex has a total interior area of 1,507 square feet (140 square meters), with a further 2,195 square feet (204 square meters) of terrace space. Although not treehouses in the most traditional sense of the term, the pods that make up Coco are suspended on their terrace well above the jungle floor, to allow the most engaging views of the spectacular site. They can thus in a very real sense be assimilated to treetop dwellings. ▪

The five pods that make up Coco are not hanging from trees but instead set up off the ground, a perfect solution for an environmentally friendly getaway on the coast of Costa Rica.

# CROW'S CASTLE

**THE CROW'S CASTLE**, or Kråkeslottet in Norwegian, is another very generous treehouse, with a floor area of 484 square feet (45 square meters) and facilities such as a shower, toilet, dishwasher, and full kitchen. It is large enough to accommodate as many as eight persons. The builders call it a "hybrid treehouse" because the cabin itself is built on the ground, where the toilet is. Lifted off the ground by a wooden frame, the second floor has a bedroom and a kitchen; the broadly glazed living room and terrace are suspended in the trees on the third level, which is 20 feet (6 meters) above the ground. The living room table and a mirror frame in the bathroom are made with the wood of a 200-year-old elm that grew nearby. Despite the comforts offered in the Crow's Castle, the overall structure has a kind of handmade aspect to it, and what seems to be a rather complex, improvised quality. Trehyttene (Three Cabins), the domain where the Crow's Castle is located, is in Gjerstad in southern Norway, about 160 miles (260 kilometers) southwest of Oslo. The forested site is near the northern end of Gjerstadvatnet lake. As witness to the widespread interest in forest lodging in Norway, there are two other equally interesting treehouses at Trehyttene called Gjøkeredet (Cuckoo's Nest) and Flåklypa. The surrounding area is well equipped for fishing, hiking, swimming, and climbing. ▪

The quirky Crow's Castle starts on the ground and works its way up into the trees, in some sense connecting the earth and the sky of southern Norway.

# CUCKOO'S NEST

**LIKE THE CROW'S CASTLE**, the Cuckoo's Nest (Gjøkeredet) is located in Gjerstad in southern Norway. It is large (387 square feet, or 36 square meters) by the standards of treehouses and it can sleep up to six persons. A full kitchen and bathroom are among the amenities. Locally sourced and milled wood was used for the structure, which has oak, birch, and larch interiors. The Cuckoo's Nest is a full 23 feet (7 meters) off the ground, and it is suspended between four pine trees. The main bedroom, with 180-degree views of the natural setting, is actually beneath the principal structure, which is somewhat unusual. A further two bunkbeds are located next to the kitchen area. An attic bedroom opens to a view of the sky. Somewhat smaller and less completely outfitted than the Crow's Castle, this treehouse nonetheless provides a gas stove in the kitchen and a woodstove for heating. Solar panels provide electricity for lighting. A wood-burning fireplace is located on the exterior balcony. These treehouses are solid, ample, and comfortable. They are, of course, like hotel suites, with the added romance of climbing up into the trees and looking down on the natural forest and lake setting. Treehouse resorts like Trehyttene, where the Cuckoo's Nest is, probably represent one of the largest sources of new construction of this type in the world—even more prevalent than individual treehouses, which might also tend to be smaller and less comfortable on the whole. Despite the features of the Norwegian treehouses seen here, they are, of course, in a (beautiful) natural setting where the real rigors of nature are quite a bit closer than they might be in a more "normal" building. ▪

Like its cousin the Crow's Castle, the Cuckoo's Nest also rises up from a firm base in the ground, but its main structure is indeed suspended in the trees, offering more modern comforts than most treehouses.

# EQUESTRIAN PARK

**THE EQUESTRIAN PARK** treehouse was built in 2019 in the Setagaya ward of Tokyo. It is a circular structure with a diameter of about 6.5 feet (2 meters). It is set nearly 25 feet (7.6 meters) above the ground and has a floor area of 323 square feet (30 square meters). It was built with Japanese elm (*Zelkova serrata*), Japanese red pine (*Pinus densiflora*), and Himalayan cedar (*Cedrus deodara*), as well as *Quercus serrata*. Because the latter is a type of oak, the theme of acorns was used in the design. Approximately three hundred wooden panels laid like thick shingles were used to create the structure, where neither nails nor screws were employed. The wood was harvested from trees that had to be cut to update the nearby Olympic venue area and fashioned in a visibly handmade way, with unaltered branches forming a railing for the interior staircase, for example. The Equestrian Park treehouse was, in fact, intended as a symbol of the Olympic site and due to be opened to the public after the events. The Baji Koen Equestrian Park was one of the venues for the 1964 Tokyo Olympics that was being adapted to host horse-related events for the games originally scheduled for 2020. This structure was designed and built by Takashi Kobayashi, a sixty-year-old former clothing buyer who became a professional treehouse builder in 1993. ▪

Though images do not reveal the real urban context of the Equestrian Park treehouse, it is located in the heart of the largest fully modern city in the world, which in itself sets it apart from other treehouses.

# FLÅKLYPA

**FLÅKLYPA IS THE** third and most recent treehouse built on the domain of Trehyttene in Gjerstad, Norway. It is set near the Cuckoo's Nest (see page 80). The proximity of Flåklypa to the Cuckoo's Nest makes it possible to imagine renting the two treehouses for a larger group. It has three levels with a ramp leading up from the ground that makes it wheelchair accessible. The structure is hung from several pine trees and includes a roof terrace 30 feet (9 meters) above the ground and a fireplace. A bedroom with a double bed gives direct access to this terrace. Flåklypa has space for up to eight people. It has some electricity supplied by solar panels, a full kitchen with a gas stove, including an oven, and a refrigerator. Locally harvested timber was used for the structure, which was assembled by carpenters based in the area. Equipped with solid wood walkways and stairs, Flåklypa looks almost like a "normal" house suspended in the trees. Its interiors are finished and decorated in what might be called a Scandinavian style. Flåklypa is clearly in the category of more sophisticated treehouses that allow city dwellers and others to have a feeling of being out in nature without necessarily giving up all the comforts of home. This has been an international trend for a number of years that has impacted not only treehouses, but other homes and places to stay in the wilderness—out in the wild, but not too far . . . ▪

Wheelchair accessible with space for up to eight persons, this treehouse combines many aspects of a more normal hotel suite, but it has a roof terrace in the trees 30 feet (9 meters) above the ground.

# HALDEN

**THE GERMAN TREEHOUSE** designer Andreas Wenning (baumraum) completed this structure in 2017. It is located in Halden, in the canton of Thurgau in the northeast of Switzerland near Lake Constance. The components of the treehouse were prefabricated in Germany and the assembly on the wooded property of the clients was carried out in just a few days. Although it is gabled, the dark gray structure sits on supports, with a 150-square-foot (14-square-meter) terrace wrapped around a single oak. The structure of the terrace is made of steel with untreated chestnut planks, and it has supports in the form of ropes and harness loops. The treehouse itself has four wooden supports and a 237-square-foot (22-square-meter) interior clad in oiled oak. Wood wool insulation is used under the exterior surfaces, which are covered in black and dark gray varnished larch. Oiled oak was also used for the built-in furniture. A black wood-burning stove provides heat as required. Looking like a miniature traditional house up in the trees from some angles, the Halden treehouse has a glass gable on the north side and other glazing that gives ample natural light to the interior. A sleeping area reached by a ladder is located above the integrated kitchenette and the bathroom, which makes use of natural stones selected from a neighboring stream for the sink and door handles. ▪

Andreas Wenning (baumraum) is clearly developing a new type of treehouse; both modern and even potentially urban, it is based on the ideas of contemporary architecture, albeit for structures that are perched above the ground.

# HALF-TREE HOUSE

**THE HALF-TREE HOUSE** was built in Barryville, New York, about 62 miles (100 kilometers) north of Manhattan, by the city-based firm JacobsChang. The black wood structure has an area of 360 square feet (33 square meters) and was built for a budget of fifty dollars per square foot. One reason for the low cost is that the structure was put together by the owners with weekend help from friends and not by a professional crew. The Half-Tree House is located on a wooded slope, and the lower end of it is supported by trees, with the entrance level resting on the ground. The connection to the trees is established using Garnier Limbs, which are engineered bolts made of high-strength steel that can be screwed into bores in tree trunks. Garnier Limbs can support weights of up to 8,000 pounds (3,600 kilograms). In this case, half of the weight of the structure is thus carried by two trees. Light and air come into the house through three floor-to-ceiling 8-by-8-foot (2.4-by-2.4-meter) pivoting steel tube windows, one of which, on the southern end, is used as the entrance. The wood selected for both the exterior and the interior is eastern pine, harvested on the 60-acre (24-hectare) property of the clients. The exterior boards were coated with Scandinavian pine tar, while the interior walls and ceiling were painted white, with clear matte sealant used on the floors. The house, which has no source of electricity or water, is equipped with a portable generator, but heat is provided by an efficient Jøtul woodstove. Like a few other structures in this book, the Half-Tree House, as its name implies, is not a pure treehouse. Anchoring one end in the earth and the other in the trees was a practical solution on the sloped, remote site. Furnishing is minimal, but the large windows offer constant and generous views of the forest. ▪

The architects and clients managed to pioneer a system where contemporary architecture and a self-build solution allow the clients to create a modern treehouse for a reasonable cost.

## LA INVERNADA

**IN REALITY, LA INVERNADA** is more of a platform in the trees than it is a treehouse. Designed by the firm GAAA (Guillermo Acuña Arquitectos Asociados), it is a 581-square-foot (54-square-meter) curved-arch house located in the forest of Curicó in central Chile. The unusual, modern design is made of locally harvested and CNC-milled laminated pine, together with 0.3-inch (8-millimeter) flexible polycarbonate sheets, partially covered with a gold-colored exterior tensile mesh membrane. Wood joints and screws were used to assemble the wood, which, of course, had been prepared off-site. On the ground floor, a wood-burning stove warms a lounge area and kitchenette. Also on the lowest level, there is a bathroom and a small bedroom that opens through glass doors to an exterior deck that surrounds an old tree. Lounge areas with pillows are located on the smaller second and third levels inside the structure. La Invernada is a remarkable example of architectural modernity in an off-grid setting in the midst of nature. Inhabitants are at once exposed to the views and light of the forest setting, but also protected in a computer-designed and milled wood and polycarbonate shell. Built in a 1,483-acre (600-hectare) private reserve, the structure, which sits on stilts, was designed to be fully reversible and non-intrusive in terms of the natural setting. "The project was conceived as an object that does not belong to the site, that can disappear at any time, and that speaks to us of the transitory condition of occupation of the forest," says the architect, Guillermo Acuña. ▪

GAAA (Guillermo Acuña Arquitectos Asociados) has pioneered a new type of forest or treehouse structure—off-grid, full of light, made largely with natural materials.

# LOFTHAVEN

**LOFTHAVEN WAS BUILT** in Spicewood, near Austin, by the Texas firm Artistree, which was founded in 2012 by the architect Will Beilharz. Influenced by the ideas of feng shui and biomimicry, Lofthaven is a circular structure inspired by traditional Mongolian yurts. The 20-foot- (6-meter-) diameter structure is located on a 26-foot- (8-meter-) diameter platform. Lofthaven is set 35 feet (10.7 meters) up in a 300-year-old bald cypress (*Taxodium distichum*) tree. It offers a 360-degree view of the limestone ravine where it is located. A bathhouse and kitchenette are situated across a creek from the treehouse. In this location, a "waterfall bathtub" was created in the rock face of the ravine. Cypress wood recovered after 2011 forest fires in the area was used for the construction. The kitchenette features a curved bar top made of peckywood cypress. The Lofthaven treehouse has a floor area of 350 square feet (32.5 square meters). It is approached via a suspended footbridge that leads to the private bathhouse. The treehouse has electricity and lighting and has an oven and a small refrigerator, but no air conditioning, given that the shade of surrounding trees keeps the area relatively cool, even in summer. A shared bathroom is located a short walk from the treehouse. It is interesting that yurts, which are more frequently anchored in the earth, inspired this structure. The efficiency of the design's round form is clear. While others found inspiration in French castles, the nomadic lifestyle of Mongolian nomads was at play here. ▪

The designer of this treehouse seems to have imagined a yurt in the sky—one of a number of innovative ideas that have emerged from this type of design in recent years.

# LÜTETSBURG

**LÜTETSBURG IS LOCATED** in northwestern Germany. Andreas Wenning was approached by the owner of the local castle, Tido Graf zu Inn- und Knyphausen, who wanted to build a treehouse in a grove near a golf course. They chose to build a "modern interpretation of the traditional gable-roof house" with anthracite-colored façades. The three wooden houses are set on steel structures that face south, lifted on stilts near the golf course and meadowland. The exterior wall cladding is in darkened larch and the roofs are in metal. A large-scale branch graphic was applied to the front glazed surfaces, in part to avoid bird collisions, but the design seems to make the buildings fit well into their forested setting. There are open terraces below and covered balconies at the end of the gables. Untreated larch was used for wall and roof interior cladding, along with gray (anthracite) fixtures. Geothermal floor heating and high-quality insulation improve the thermal and energy performance of the houses. Each has a kitchenette, dining table, lounge area, and Wi-Fi access. Open galleries on the upper level with views of the countryside are intended for sleeping. The Lütetsburg treehouses have steel structures with vertical and oblique steel supports. The lower terraces are 9.8 feet (3 meters) above the ground, living space is at 13.8 feet (4.2 meters), and sleeping space at 22.3 feet (6.8 meters). ▪

It is interesting to note that a number of very contemporary treehouse designs take on the often practiced typologies of residential architecture—in this case a typical gable-roof house.

# MADRONE GROVE

**THE MADRONE GROVE** Equilibrium Home treehouse is in Woodside, California. It was completed in May 2019 by Dustin Feider and his firm, O2. It is built, like the Prairie Treehouse and Banana Slug Mountain, in California redwood (*Sequoia sempervirens*) and rises from 10 to 25 feet (3 to 7.6 meters) above ground level. Its floor area is 200 square feet (18.5 square meters). It features a sleeping loft and a slide down from the stairs. It was built with redwood and Douglas fir together with prefabricated birch plywood panels. The treehouse is reached by a solid wooden staircase. Inside it is bright and inviting, with large, glazed surfaces, including the entrance door. Anchored to large trees, the Madrone Grove structure appears, especially from a distance, to be quite traditional in its design, in particular because of its simplicity. Nonetheless, it is based on modern building techniques, a fact visible from the triangulated supporting frame that allows the building to seem almost to float between the trees, and surely also the large windows. Feider is somewhat of an exception amongst treehouse designers precisely because of his ability to combine or alternate very modern structures with more "normal"-looking wooden buildings perched high above the ground. ▪

Contemporary building techniques allow treehouses to conquer new heights and to offer larger floor areas than their predecessors, while still calling on traditional materials like wood.

# MIMOSA

**THE MIMOSA TREEHOUSE** was built on Kangaroo Island, Australia, in 2014. Kangaroo Island is a forty-five-minute ferry ride southwest of Adelaide. The octagonal structure has a diameter of 13 feet (4 meters) and a height of more than 21 feet (6.5-meters). Set 23 feet (7 meters) off the ground, it was built using eucalyptus, birch, and ironwood. Its floor area is 300 square feet (28 square meters). Because of the location, the design assumes an almost circular form to channel high winds. A 2020 wildfire left the structure untouched. The unusual, dynamic design is by the self-trained Japanese treehouse architect Takashi Kobayashi. The rather complex configuration is woven into its host tree, but also uses stilts to generate the required support. A unique feature of the interior living space is that a large surface of the eucalyptus itself is made visible where the smoother wall splits open. Although his work may not be quite as whimsical as that of Terunobu Fujimori, Kobayashi certainly shares with the older architect a very marked sense of the relationship of nature to his designs. Mimosa is not only in a tree, but it also seems literally to become part of its twisting branches. A wood-burning stove provides warmth, although there is electricity in the structure. Long oblique windows rise around the main living space, which is set beneath a rooftop terrace. ▪

Takashi Kobayashi is one of the most original designers of treehouses in the world. His strength is an ability to meld nature and a sense of architecture, carried high into the trees.

# MONKEY HOUSE

**THE MONKEY HOUSE** was built in Paraty in the state of Rio de Janeiro in 2020 by the São Paulo architect Marko Brajovic. Brajovic was inspired by the reappearance of capuchin monkeys in the mountainous terrain, which is at the border of the state of São Paulo. His Monkey House has a 16-square-foot (1.5-square-meter) footprint and was built with interlocking wooden components covered by Galvalume (zinc, aluminum, and silicon) skin and thermo-acoustic insulation. The architect looked to the forms of an endemic palm tree called juçara (*Euterpe edulis*), which anchors itself in sloping terrain, for this structure. He says, "For the Monkey House we implemented the same strategy, creating a series of thin and dense pillars, inspired by the morphology of the roots of the juçara palm, thus ensuring stability of the vertical construction." The vertical design includes two bedrooms that can be made into lounge space separate from the kitchen and bathroom. There are terraces on the two sides and another on the top floor. The naturally ventilated Monkey House has an area of 581 square feet (54 square meters), with a further 344 square feet (32 square meters) of covered space that is in direct contact with the forest environment. Bamboo interiors and curtains made from locally sourced fishing nets complement Japanese design objects and indigenous Guarani handicraft pieces. Brajovic also did the landscape design for the project, privileging native plants. ▪

Using modern materials, the creator of this treehouse sought to inspire himself from the natural forms of the site. The design also calls on Japanese and Guarani design.

_Roderick Wolgamott and Romero Studios / Wolgamott Works_

# MYSTIC TREEHOUSE

**LOCATED IN MYSTIC,** Connecticut, the Mystic Treehouse was designed and built by Roderick Wolgamott and Romero Studios/Wolgamott Works. The site is on a 400-acre (162-hectare) farm in a forest area where beech, silver birch, maple, and oak trees grow. The structure offers 500 square feet (46.5 square meters) of interior space with a further 150-square-foot (14-square-meter) deck. The materials used were in good part sourced by the Oregon firm TerraMai and include wood salvaged from barns in Brazil. The stairway was built using gathered driftwood from the northeastern United States. The deck of the structure is a substantial 40 feet (12 meters) above the ground. Wolgamott started his firm in New York in 1997 and has built more than fifty treehouses around the world, some for very well-known clients. A crew of six persons built the Mystic Treehouse over a four-week period in 2017. The result very definitely has a handmade quality and, indeed, a kind of artistic presence that is expressed in the woodworking and accumulation of different kinds of branches and wood and the very real warmth of the interiors. ∎

Roderick Wolgamott makes use of natural materials and calls on his personal artistic sense to create treehouses that are entirely connected to their woodland sites and are imbued with originality.

# THE NEST

**THE NEST WAS BUILT** in Austin, Texas, by Will Beilharz and his firm, Artistree. It is rather unusually large for a treehouse at 600 square feet (56 square meters) and includes several bedrooms and a kitchen. Beilharz says, "We focused on 'up-cycling' and biomimicry as the main construction concepts. Much of the material used to build the Nest is reclaimed from our own property or up-cycled—from the floors in the bedrooms to the mason jars used for drinking glasses." The kitchen has window trim made of black walnut from the property and a cypress table milled on-site. Recycled cider casks were used for the wall in the main bedroom. The unusual design, with its suspended structure, walkways, and platforms, lies in a limestone ravine under an over-arching metal grid meant to encourage the growth of flowering vines. Although the photos here do not show significant plant covering, the designers count on nature to provide a new habitat for insects and birds above the aptly named Nest. Whereas most treehouses seek their inspiration in the world of architecture (mostly traditional), the Nest has an air of refuge about it, perhaps refuge from the apocalypse, but there is a sense here not only of being in nature, but of becoming part of it, which is very attractive. The finishing and design are in keeping with the "up-cycle" style wanted by Beilharz—a certain irregularity coupled with a good level of comfort and the literally surrounding presence of nature. ▪

Calling on upcycling and biomimicry, the designer has imagined a broader, more inclusive kind of treehouse that also calls on the ideas of modern architecture.

# ORIGIN

**DESIGNED BY THE** Paris-based studio Lavit, Origin was built in a 100-year-old oak at the Château de Raray in the Oise area of northern France in 2017. The inspiration of the architects was quite simply the accumulated branches that form bird nests. The access to the treehouse is via a platform with a thermal spa in another tree 98 feet (30 meters) away. A wooden ladder leads up to a roof terrace that offers a 360-degree view of the forest setting. The octagonal design with two large sliding-glass doors envelops the oak. The wood used for the exterior cladding is horizontally stacked Douglas fir. The patio terrace and the panoramic terrace are in larch wood, while on the interior, wall and ceiling cladding is in poplar. The entrance gives way to a living space and a sleeping area, while a narrow corridor has three sliding doors that conceal a dressing room, a bathroom with a shower and toilet, and technical space. Origin has a floor area of 248 square feet (23 square meters). The overall impression of this house, despite its natural inspiration, is quite modern, both inside and out. Running water and electricity are integrated into the structure, creating a comfortable environment despite being 36 feet (11 meters) off the ground. The Château de Raray is now a hotel with more traditional rooms. The treehouses are in a forest that overlooks the golf course and are part of a complex of structures called Coucoo Grands Chênes, which is an independent organization. ▪

The inspiration of nature is very often the driving force behind treehouses, but, in this instance, the designer gives that inspiration a modern form—a kind of architectural riff on bird nests.

# PIGNA

**DESIGNED BY THE** architect Claudio Beltrame, Pigna is located in Malborghetto, near the border of Austria and Slovenia in northeastern Italy. Built in 2017, the two structures each have an area of 377 square feet (35 square meters). Beltrame and his son Luca imagined treehouses that would "represent the forest" that surrounds their hometown. The first structure is set 13 feet (4 meters) above the ground and serves as a "panoramic covered terrace," whereas the second, equally rounded structure, mimicking the imagined profile of a pinecone (*pigna*) has two large windows or sliding doors. A living room with a rough-hewn wooden couch faces a small kitchen and a bathroom. Stairs lead from there to the upper-level bedroom. The double bed is placed beneath a round skylight at the very top of the treehouse. The structure was made out of CLT (cross-laminated timber), insulated with wood fiber and then covered with larch shingles that turn gray when exposed to humidity and sunlight. The architect explains that the small shingles make it easier to follow the curvature of the treehouses. As with any larch-clad structure, Pigna's original light color has slowly faded to gray, making it blend almost entirely into its wooded environment. ▪

Claudio Beltrame used the pinecone as the inspiration for the form of these related treehouses.

CLT wood and natural materials reinforce the connection to the forest.

# PLAYA VIVA

**PLAYA VIVA WAS BUILT** mostly from local materials in 2015 in Zihuatanejo, Mexico, which is in the southern state of Guerrero. It is part of a beachfront luxury eco-resort and is suspended 6 feet (1.8 meters) above the ground in palm trees. The trees pierce the clay tile roof of the structure. Designed by Will Beilharz and his firm, Artistree, the treehouse has a net hammock that is suspended in a floor opening and overlooks the ocean. It also has a king-size bed. A bathroom is located on a separate platform and is clad inside in locally made tiles. The rounded, bundled bamboo form of the structure opens fully on both ends, offering views of the ocean, and includes a side terrace wrapped around a palm tree. Smaller side windows open like hatches with rope handles, and a large, curved, sliding entry door gives an impression of privacy despite the overall openness of the house. The entire suite has an ample floor area of 700 square feet (65 square meters) and was built in just six months from design initiation to receiving the first guests. Water used by the suite is heated with solar energy and recycled where possible. ▪

The unusual tubelike structure of this elevated house (in the trees) makes it ideal as beachside accommodation with all the comforts in an eco-resort.

# PRAIRIE TREEHOUSE

**LIKE THE OTHER O2** treehouses published in this volume (Banana Slug Mountain, Madrone Grove), the Prairie Treehouse Equilibrium Home is located in Woodside, California, and was completed in 2018. It is also lodged in California redwoods (*Sequoia sempervirens*) and was built using redwood, Douglas fir, and birch plywood panels assembled on the O2 proprietary Tetratruss frame. The prefabricated wall panels echo the geometry of the struts that support the house. This is, in fact, the third such structure dubbed "Equilibrium" that O2 has completed. It has a floor area of 200 square feet (18.5 square meters) and was built 30 feet (9 meters) above ground. The house features electrical power and a compost toilet, as well as an independent exterior terrace, dubbed the "sky porch" by the designer, which is reached by a wooden skybridge suspended from steel cables that has wraparound benches and a barbecue. Once again, this treehouse, which is somewhat less contemporary in appearance than other O2 creations, reveals its modernity immediately when seen from below—with the triangulated wooden supports. This design does bring to mind something of the work of Buckminster Fuller. As the founder of O2, Dustin Feider, puts it, "I was really fascinated with the idea of building a kit-style treehouse that can fit in any tree. That was the original design criteria when I built a geodesic dome in the backyard of my dad's home. Buckminster Fuller is a huge inspiration to me. I just had this big vision, traveling and building kit-style treehouses . . . around the world." ▪

The triangulated struts that mark the bottom of this treehouse are the sign of its links to modern engineering and architecture, even as its wooden forms allow it to connect to the forest.

# SACRED FOREST

**THE 100-SQUARE-FOOT** (9.3-square-meter) Sacred Forest treehouse was built by O2 in 2018 in Woodside, California. It is set 20 feet (6.1 meters) off the ground. Set amid California redwoods (*Sequoia sempervirens*), the structure was built with redwood and Douglas fir. Redwood tongue-and-groove boarding is combined with Plexiglas and polycarbonate windows and roof. The single-slope roof offers guests a chance literally to look up at the trees from a bunk-style bed, or even closer to touch the bark of the redwood around which the treehouse was built. This realization is something of a return to a more traditional (i.e., smaller and less outfitted with modern comforts) type of treehouse, even if the polycarbonate roof is distinctively modern. The type of structure concerned would seem ideal for someone who, perhaps even alone, wishes really to get away from the modern world. Furnishing is minimal, as is appropriate in such a small volume. A steep wooden ladder leads from the forest floor through a hatched opening in the small terrace opposite the fully glazed entrance. ▪

A return to a more "traditional" type of treehouse after many efforts to modernize the genre, the Sacred Forest treehouse is also immersed in what might be considered a primeval forest.

# THE 7TH ROOM

**THE TREEHOTEL**, located in Harads in northern Sweden, has become a reference for treehouse design. Several architects have already participated in the creation of individual rooms, all perched in the tall pines of the site. The 7th Room is located 33 feet (10 meters) above the ground with a view of treetops and the Lule River in the distance. A staircase for guests and a small lift for luggage are part of the design. To reduce the strain on the trees in which the 7th Room was built, twelve columns were added to carry the greater part of the weight. As in a traditional Nordic cabin, the wooden façade is clad with dark (burnt) pine boards. Floors indoors are made of ash wood, and birch is used for the interior walls. This suite in the trees includes two bedrooms, a lounge, a bathroom, and a terrace and can accommodate up to five persons. There are two floor levels in the structure, with a one-foot difference between them. The lounge area is on the lower floor, while the bedrooms are on the upper level with the beds embedded in the floor. The lounge has a central pellet stove and simple furniture, such as a Scandia chair by the Norwegian designer Hans Brattrud. The bedrooms are located on opposite sides of the cabin, facing the central tree and netted terrace, with large sliding-glass doors to go out onto the net. The structure was designed by the reputed Oslo firm Snøhetta and has a floor area of 592 square feet (55 square meters). ▪

Snøhetta is one of the better-known international architecture firms, and the fact that they have become involved in treehouse designs is an indication of the broad success of the genre.

# SNAKE HOUSES

**DESIGNED BY THE** Lisbon firm Rebelo de Andrade, the Snake Houses were completed in 2015 in Vila Pouca de Aguiar, in northern Portugal. The architects write, "The Snake Houses most undoubtedly bring to mind one's childhood and its heritage of dreams. Who never wished to have a treehouse, or never to grow old, like Peter Pan? The Snake Houses, built on piles and rejecting all right angles, emerge quietly from among the treetops. The materials—slate and wood—that cover them enhance the desired effect of concealment." The long, thin structures touch ground at the narrower entrance ramp and rise on three oblique metal stilts over the forest floor at the far end, which is the location of the bed and two large windows, one facing the natural setting and the other, the sky. The interior finishing can be described as modern and efficient—the real drama of the structures lies in their unusual plan and external appearance. Each 237-square-foot (22-square-meter) house has a sitting area, a double bed, a television, a bathroom, and a kitchen. They are air-conditioned in summer and have Wi-Fi connections. The Snake Houses are part of the Pedras Salgadas Spa & Nature Park, where Luis Rebelo de Andrade also created eco-houses and a cottage; the cottage includes a thermal spa by Álvaro Siza. ▪

The unusual narrow form of the aptly named Snake Houses is another take on the modernization of the typical treehouse, here lifted off the ground on stilts and not actually supported by trees.

# THE SPIRAL (TREEFUL)

**THE SPIRAL TREEHOUSE** has a staircase that winds up its host tree to an overall height of 35 feet (10.7 meters) and has a floor area of 248 square feet (23 square meters). It is in Nago, in the north of the Japanese island of Okinawa, which has a subtropical climate. The Spiral overlooks the Genka River—reputed to have some of the cleanest water in Japan and is part of the Treeful Treehouse Sustainable Resort, which opened in 2021. Three other treehouses are located on the site. Equipped with air conditioning, the Spiral has 360-degree views of its forest setting and includes an outdoor terrace with a hammock. Treehouse residents share a modern structure called the Aerohouse, which has bathrooms and rest and relaxation rooms, as well as a kitchen. The different structures are connected by a catwalk whose forms are inspired by vertebrae, providing access to handicapped persons, as Japanese legislation often requires. The resort is powered by solar energy and its founders, Satoru and Maha Kikugawa, participate in local projects, such as the renovation of a water mill that sits beside the nearby Shizogumui Waterfall. The area allows for kayaking, paddle-boarding, and jungle trekking. ▪

The Spiral evokes the kind of original treehouse that made this type of structure so popular across the world—it is dreamy and really wrapped around a tree.

# TREE DRAGON

**TREE DRAGON WAS** built in Higashi-Matsushima in the prefecture of Miyagi, Japan. On March 11, 2011, Higashi-Matsushima saw two-thirds of its buildings destroyed by the so-called Tohoku earthquake and tsunami and suffered over one thousand deaths out of a population of about 40,000 persons. The treehouse was built by Takashi Kobayashi in 2013 as a symbol of the post-disaster reconstruction and as a place of prayer for those who suffered losses in 2011. Rising to a total height of 30 feet (9 meters) off the ground, the structure has a floor area of 323 square feet (35 square meters) disposed on three levels. It was built in a Japanese hackberry (*Celtis sinensis* var. *japonica*) on a steeply sloped site. This unexpected location led the designer to carve the 129-square-foot (12-square-meter) ground floor out of the slope to form a "cave" with a stone fireplace inside. The exterior is covered with sliced disks of wood, and the roof of the treehouse is partially shingled. The next floor up is an open platform with natural stripped wood used to form the railings and supports. The top, smallest level measures 5 by 6.5 feet (1.5 by 2 meters), and with its unexpected 9-foot- (2.7-meter-) high organically formed open shell contributes to the overall impression that this entire structure is, indeed, a place of prayer, firmly anchored in its natural setting. The name of the treehouse is also evoked in the way that it appears almost to crawl up the hillside. ▪

The idea of making an obviously light and ephemeral structure into a symbol after the destruction wrought by the 2011 Tohoku earthquake may well be an indication of the direction that architecture should go in the future.

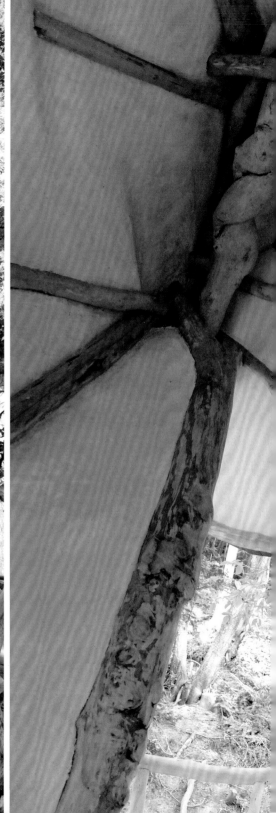

# WHITE OAKS

**WHITE OAKS WAS** built in Washington, Connecticut, in 2018 by Roderick Wolgamott and his firm, Romero Studios/Wolgamott Works with a crew of four in just four weeks. The main part of the structure is set 30 feet (9 meters) above the ground in five white oak trees that make their appearance in the midst of the decks. The area of White Oaks is a generous 600 square feet (56 square meters), with a further 150 square feet (14 square meters) of decks. The designer explains, "The stairway leads to a covered bridge, which is connected by a sculptural nest made of 2,500 feet (762 meters) of indigenous vines." These vines give the approach to the house an unexpected, but artistic feeling, which is echoed in the variety of wooden surfaces of the house itself. The house was built entirely with reclaimed or salvaged wood from a barn that was dismantled in upstate New York. The interiors benefit from large, glazed areas that give a feeling of proximity to nature, even as, together with the woodwork, they convey an impression of quality construction. There are also unexpected artistic touches, such as a series of small round colored-glass windows in the eaves. The relatively flat grassy setting of White Oaks makes for a comfortable natural environment enlivened by such features as a long, hand-laid stone wall. Wolgamott shows an unusual ability to combine a natural, sometimes almost organic design with a treehouse that recalls a reduced version of a real residence, albeit one perched in the trees. ▪

The artistry of Roderick Wolgamott might well, for some, bring to mind the work of the artist Andy Goldsworthy with a practical aspect added on—here branches become a treehouse that is a work of art.

# WILLOW

**DESIGNED BY ANTONY GIBBON,** who was trained as a furniture designer, this trapezoidal structure might better be described as an elevated home rather than a treehouse. It is built on stilts, touching the ground at three points in a forested site near a lake in the Catskills near Woodstock, New York, and measures a comfortable 560 square feet (52 square meters). The Willow treehouse has both water and electricity that are run down from the main house on this private property. It was built with locally and sustainably sourced timber and has reclaimed, FSC-certified pine interiors. The exteriors are clad in reclaimed cedar, reused from an old house in the region. The main area inside is an open-plan lounge space that includes a wood-burning stove and a kitchen. A large rectangular window looks out toward the lake, giving residents a full view of the natural surroundings. A loft bedroom reached by a ladder is on the upper level. A second bedroom and shower are located to the rear of the building, which has balconies on either side. The area below the elevated volume offers a further terrace space leading to a hot tub. The designer explains, "New trees were also planted close to the structure to help strengthen the idea that the building cuts through the forest and is semi-camouflaged into its surroundings. The sharp geometric angles of the interior also created an interesting layout that pushed away from 90-degree corners as much as possible." Willow might well be an indication of just how broadly the actual definition of treehouses has spread in recent years. Though it is, of course, not technically suspended from trees, it is very much amongst the trees and lifted off the ground. Gibbon has said that his work is often "a fusion of luxury lifestyle . . . with the rustic outdoor experience." ▪

Willow is another take on the modernization of treehouses—again, not actually hanging in the trees, but quite definitely sitting above its natural setting.

# WOODNEST

**WOODNEST WAS BUILT** in 2020 on a steep, forested site near Odda, Norway, by the architects Helen & Hard, who have offices in Stavanger and Oslo. The two structures are suspended between 16 and 20 feet (5 and 6 meters) above the ground, attached using steel collars to single pine trees. The treehouses have floor areas of just 161 square feet (15 square meters). Because of the careful designs, it is possible to sleep four persons in the structures, and also to have a bathroom, kitchen space, and living area. The architects explain, "Inspired by the Norwegian cultural traditions of vernacular timber architecture, together with a desire to experiment with the material potential of wood, the architecture is structurally supported by the tree trunk itself and formed from a series of radial glulam timber ribs. The untreated natural timber shingles encase the volume, creating a protective skin around the building, which will weather over time to merge and blend with the natural patina of the surrounding forest." Approached by long wooden ramps, the shingled structures have ample windows that frame spectacular views of the Hardangerfjord. ▪

Treehouses that are actually designed by architects may be the exception, but they do tend to break new ground and to help to redefine this popular building type.

| *Guy Mallinson and Keith Brownlie of Brownlie Ernst and Marks (BEaM)*

# WOODSMAN'S TREEHOUSE

THE APPROACH TO THIS treehouse located in Dorset is a raised timber walkway and a suspension bridge that leads to a charred oak door and stacked log walls. It is wrapped around an English oak but is structurally independent from the host tree. The design was a collaboration between the owner, Guy Mallinson, and Keith Brownlie of the Dorset bridge designers Brownlie Ernst and Marks (BEaM). Woodsman's Treehouse won the 2017 RIBA South West Small Project of the Year award. The RIBA jury commented, "The project displays a masterly control of form and function, with pinches of references from Borromini, Palladio, and Stirling. All this squeezed into a tiny first project for this relatively new practice specifically formed to design bridges anywhere in the world. The promise of this level of innovation in the world of bridge design is a nice thought!" The 377-square-foot (35-square-meter) treehouse is a luxurious two-story suite arranged as a central cylinder within a rectilinear exterior. A large copper bathtub is set into a glass-backed space with a massive oak trunk rising behind it. The designer explains, "A rusticated top sits on the rotunda roof—inverting the tradition of a rusticated base, in the absence of any base to rusticate. The rooftop sauna box, clad in larch slab wood with elongated waterspouts and slit windows, gives the unmistakable impression of a defensive position, a treetop fort keeping guard over the treehouse and the pier that connects it back to *terra firma*." The central octagonal form of the treehouse is clad with alternating strips of Douglas fir and cedar. On the exterior, the upper deck has a sauna and hot tub, while the lower features an open-air tree shower, hammock, wood-fired pizza oven, barbecue, and slide that leads down to the forest floor. Woodsman's Treehouse is in Malllinson's Woodland Retreat in Holditch, Chard, 11.6 miles (18.7 kilometers) northwest of Bridport. ▪

244

| Not many treehouses win RIBA awards, but this is one. | References to architectural history abound as do | unexpected comforts such as a rooftop sauna. |

# YOKI

**THE YOKI TREEHOUSE** was built in Austin, Texas by Will Beilharz (Artistree) between two old bald cypress (*Taxodium distichum*) trees in 2018. The 600-square-foot (56-square-meter) structure is set 25 feet (7.6 meters) above a creek. The designer explains that *yoki* is a Hopi Native American word for rain. Yoki is connected to a separated bathhouse via a 60-foot (18-meter) suspension bridge. The treehouse is entered from its second-level observation deck, from which a spiral staircase leads down to the rounded front terrace that is penetrated by two trunks from the same tree. The interior, with its front wall of windows, is clad in birch wood. The living area has a couch facing the view and a table near the kitchenette. A ladder leads up to an extra bed perched on a kind of independent mezzanine. The main bedroom with its queen-size bed is at the rear of the structure. The furnishing and decor of the Yoki treehouse are relatively minimal and modern, allowing guests to appreciate the forest setting more fully. Perched on a metallic truss, the treehouse has a modern appearance, accentuated by the generous vertical and horizontal bands of glazing. The fact that it is in the trees, and above a stream, makes the connection with nature even more powerful. ▪

Will Beilharz mixes a real interest in treehouses with a scale and level of complexity rarely seen hanging 25 feet (7.6 meters) above the ground. A metallic truss is mixed with wooden volumes.

PAGE 1
Black Crystal,
near Woodstock,
New York, USA

PAGES 2-3
La Invernada,
Curicó, Chile

PAGES 4-5
Coco, Uvita,
Costa Rica

PAGES 6-7
Woodnest,
near Odda,
Norway

First published in the United States of America in 2022 by
Rizzoli International Publications, Inc.

300 Park Avenue South
New York, NY 10010
www.rizzoliusa.com

Ellen R. Cohen, Editor
Kaija Markoe, Production Manager
Design by Sarah Gifford

Copyright © Rizzoli International Publications
Text: Philip Jodidio
Preface: Emily Nelson

ISBN: 978-0-8478-6961-9
Library of Congress Control Number: 2021944390

Printed in China

2022 2023 2024 2025 2026 / 10 9 8 7 6 5 4 3 2 1

## PHOTOGRAPH CREDITS

**AIR CASTLE** (pp. 18, 20–25): *Urnatur*

**ANANDA** (pp. 9, 26–31): *Josh Herbert Photography*

**BANANA SLUG MOUNTAIN** (pp. 32–37): *Dustin Feider*

**BIRD HUT** (pp. 38–43): *Studio North*

**BLACK CRYSTAL** (pp. 1, 44–49): *Andreas Wenning of baumraum*

**CABANE HAUTEFORT** (pp. 50–53): *Châteaux dans les Arbres*

**CHÂTEAU MILANDES** (pp. 54–59): *Châteaux dans les Arbres*

**THE CINDER CONE** (pp. 60–65): *Foster Huntington*

**COCO** (pp. 4–5, 66–73): *BoysPlayNice*

**CROW'S CASTLE** (pp. 74–79): *Åse Kristine Mæsel Trydal*

**CUCKOO'S NEST** (pp. 80–87): *Åse Kristine Mæsel Trydal*

**EQUESTRIAN PARK** (pp. 88–93): *Takashi Koboyashi*

**FLÅKLYPA** (pp. 94–99): *Åse Kristine Mæsel Trydal*

**HALDEN** (pp. 100–107): *Andreas Wenning of baumraum*

**HALF-TREE HOUSE** (pp. 108–13): *Noah Kalina*

**LA INVERNADA** (pp. 2–3, 114–21): *Estudio Palma*

**LOFTHAVEN** (pp. 122–27): *Eric Shlegel*: pp. 125, 126, 127

**LÜTETSBURG** (pp. 128–33): *Andreas Wenning of baumraum*

**MADRONE GROVE** (pp. 134–39): *O2 Treehouse*

**MIMOSA** (pp. 140–45): *Maha Kikugawa*

**MONKEY HOUSE** (pp. 146–51): *Rafael Medeiros, Gustavo Uemura*

**MYSTIC TREEHOUSE** (pp. 152–57): *Diedre Kraimer*

**THE NEST** (pp. 158–65): *ArtisTree*

**ORIGIN** (pp. 166–73): *Atelier Lavit*

**PIGNA** (pp. 174–81): *Claudio Beltrame*

**PLAYA VIVA** (pp. 182–89): *Artistree Home, Kev Steele*; *Smiling Forest Photography*, p. 13

**PRAIRIE TREEHOUSE** (pp. 190–95): *O2 Treehouse*

**SACRED FOREST** (pp. 196–99): *O2 Treehouse*

**THE 7TH ROOM** (pp. 200–205): *Snøhetta*

**SNAKE HOUSES** (pp. 206–13): *Rebelo de Andrade*

**THE SPIRAL (TREEFUL)** (pp. 214–19): *Maha Kikugawa*

**TREE DRAGON** (pp. 16, 220–25): *Takashi Koboyashi*

**WHITE OAKS** (pp. 226–31): *Kevin Ellis*

**WILLOW** (pp. 10, 232–37): *M. Dimitrov, Moriarti Photography*

**WOODNEST** (pp. 6–7, 15, 238–43): *Alek Pérez*, pp. 238–39; *Tor Hveem*, p. 240; *Sindre Ellingsen*, p. 241; *Tor Hveem & Gjermund photography*, pp. 6–7, 242

**WOODSMAN'S TREEHOUSE** (pp. 244–49): *Sandy Steele-Perkins*

**YOKI** (pp. 250–55) *ArtisTree: Cynthia Carvajal*, pp. 251, 254, 255 (top), 255 (bottom); *Erich Schlegel*, pp. 252–53